RAILWAY
·HALSGROVE·
SERIES

LAST DAYS OF STEAM
WESTERN & SOUTHERN

Tony Butcher

HALSGROVE

ACKNOWLEDGEMENTS

I must mention my wife Anne, whose excellent typing
has been essential to this and previous ventures, as well as her
understanding and support over the years to my lifetime obsession.

First published in Great Britain in 2014

Copyright © Tony Butcher 2014

British Library Cataloguing-in-Publication Data
A CIP record for this title is available from the British Library

ISBN 978 0 85704 226 2

HALSGROVE

Halsgrove House,
Ryelands Industrial Park,
Bagley Road, Wellington, Somerset TA21 9PZ
Tel: 01823 653777   Fax: 01823 216796
email: sales@halsgrove.com

Part of the Halsgrove group of companies.
Information on all Halsgrove titles is available at: www.halsgrove.com

Printed and bound in China by Everbest Printing Co Ltd

Title page image: Light Bulleid Pacifics Nos.34102 "Lapford"
and No.34057 "Biggin Hill" run through the already closed
station of Grateley with the LCGB "Bridport Belle" rail tour
of 22/1/67, en route to Westbury. Here modified West
Country Class No.34013 took over to take the GWR route to
Maiden Newton for a visit to the Bridport Branch behind two
Ivatt 2-6-2Ts. Unfortunately with a change to wet weather the
two tanks proved unable to climb the steep bank up from
Powerstock on the return from Bridport, and after several
failed attempts stalled at the bottom of the bank, and had to
finally be rescued by a diesel locomotive in the fast fading
light. By then the tour was running several hours late.

INTRODUCTION

Like many, my first interest in railways was focused on model railways and obtaining my first Hornby Dublo Set. In the early years after the war such things were in very short supply. My father managed to get a 'Sir Nigel Gresley' Set, which he said was about the only one left in London. Some years later, however a cousin of thirteen came to stay with us for a week. His father and brother were also very keen on railways, and his father had large OO and O gauge layouts. To keep my young visitor occupied during the week I took him up to Clapham Junction to do some train-spotting, and my interest in the real thing was reawakened. I had been given a basic camera for my birthday, and I began taking a few black and white photographs. However, the camera was severely limited by having a maximum shutter speed of 1/75 sec. I then progressed to a relatively cheap 2¼ x 3¼ Kodak camera, which I bought with money from delivering parcels at Christmas for the Post Office in 1956. This at least had a 1/200 second shutter, and I did start to take some reasonable pictures in 1956.

During the late '50s I went round most of the Southern sheds, although as a student I had no car or motorbike in those days, so this was all by public transport – largely on the trains. I did obtain official shed permits for most of the sheds from Waterloo Head Office, and had to fit the dates to my holidays, etc., depending on where they were located

My action photography started at Surbiton (in those days you could see the whole 'Lord Nelson' class in a day, unless one happened to be in works) and along the North Downs on the Redhill – Reading line. The Redhill – Guildford line still had the last of the SECR D class 4-4-0s running along the North Downs, as well as the odd T9, Q, Q1 etc. apart from the usual Southern Moguls. In addition there was a daily Western Region engine working from Reading and back in the earlier years with a 43XX 2-6-0 and later a Manor 4-6-0. On some mornings I managed to slip away from my workplace in Redhill or Dorking to photograph the return working to Reading. There were also the summer Saturday through trains from the South Coast to the Midlands hauled usually by the relatively new Standard Class 4 2-6-0s.

Although the Southern Region had the smallest number of steam locomotives by a long way, it still possessed in this period a surprising number of interesting classes, including many of very old vintage. The M7 and E4 tanks (both introduced in 1897), as well as the H tanks (used on the Central & SE sections of the Southern), particularly come to mind. There were still considerable numbers of these operating in the latter half of the 1950s (e.g. 61 E4s, 57 Hs and 103 M7s in the summer of 1956). There were also several classes of 4-4-0s still surviving, including classes D (only to 1956), D1, L, L1, E1 and T9, all very good looking engines. Many old classes of tank engines still survived initially from 1956 onwards in small numbers, such as E1, B4, 0395 (Adams 1874), 0415 (Adams Radial 1882) as well as the well loved Beattie well tanks dating from 1874 and A1/A1X originally of 1872 vintage! This is not to mention small classes of older main line engines still in use like the beautiful Brighton Atlantics

I guess that the survival of so many old engines was partly due to having to be retained during the Second World War and its austerity aftermath, and also because the Southern had a large amount of the region already electrified in the 1930s. The latter meant that the Southern did not need such a large fleet of main line engines as the other Regions, although Maunsell Lord Nelsons and King Arthurs were still very much in evidence. The elimination of steam in the South Eastern Section in June 1961, due to further electrification to the Kent Coast, did of course then hasten the end of many of these interesting old classes.

A further period followed during which I took black and white shots of everyday steam, within the limits of not having my own transport and studying at university. By this time I had graduated to an Agfa Isolette 2 square camera with a 1/500 sec shutter. It was a good little bellows camera, but it did suffer from some drop-off in definition on the left hand side at larger apertures.

Having lived in the South East all my life until then, I naturally became first and foremost a 'Southern Man' with my railway interest and photography. However, my next nearest region was the Western. Like the Southern Region it was remarkable to think how one could see a whole succession of 'Kings', 'Castles' and all other main line 4-6-0s in less than a day's photography on the Great Western main line out of London to which I made a number of forays. Also on the main line to Birmingham the 'Kings' could be seen on hourly services in 1962. After that they were all gone, apart from one No.6018 which was held over to work a farewell special in April 1962. GWR steam finished quite early. 1964 was the last year that one could see a fair quantity of Great Western engines still working. A limited number of engines held out until 1965, but usually in a very dirty state usually lacking a nameplate, smokebox number plate etc. It was a sad time to see the end of GWR locomotives on British Railways, except for a couple of operational preserved engines such as "Clun Castle" and "Pendennis Castle," employed on specials.

From the end of 1958 my time was taken up with getting married, finding a house and starting my first job, which rather put an end to my railway activities for three years.

I did manage to start photographing steam engines again from mid 1961 when I then obtained my first 35mm camera fitted with a good 50mm lens and range finder focusing. I continued to take only black and white until 1962, when I started to take some colour pictures in 2¼in square format, both colour negatives and transparencies. However, these were taken with a very basic Kodak camera belonging to my wife. It was not until mid-1963 that I started taking 35mm colour transparencies; by then the Beeching report was starting to take effect, and many of the engines were dirty and unkempt. Furthermore, many of the famous classes (e.g. 'King', 'Princess Royal', 'Schools', 'Lord Nelson', 'King Arthur', un-rebuilt 'Patriot') had been fully withdrawn at the end of 1962. I still, however, continued to take mainly black and white photographs throughout the BR years and only principally took colour in the last years of British steam from 1965 to '68.

This situation awakened my photographic interest in railway enthusiast specials, for which the locomotives were normally very well turned out and were often the last survivors of classes that could by then be seen only with difficulty if at all in normal service. My holiday leave in those days was severely limited to three weeks and had to include my wife's holiday; that almost all these specials ran at weekends was therefore a big plus. A good steam tour had many attractions, all concentrated into the few hours available. The routes chosen, often circular in nature, were usually of particular interest, traversing little used cross country lines, freight only branches and many other delightful branches of the pre-Beeching type.

Often, of course, the weather was not good, and efforts to capture the shots on 50 ASA Agfa colour transparency film were not always very successful. Partly because of this I continued taking a lot of black and white shots up to the end of BR steam, initially on 35mm FP3 film and latterly on 2¼inch FP3 and 400 ASA TRIX, the latter much the more useful in dull weather. 35mm 25 ASA Kodachrome, although the best film, was usually used only in sunny weather because of its low speed. In fact looking back at my black and white work, I am surprised on occasions to see how well a shot has come out, even though the weather was very poor, which would have been hopeless for colour in those non-digital days.

However, I have always liked black and white photography. I have always done all my own developing and printing over the years. In this digital age I actually find it quite pleasant to spend a couple of hours in the darkroom, and to this day have still been doing some printing with my enlarger. Perhaps also black and white photographs of the BR steam age give a more nostalgic and historic impression than colour of the "Great Days of Steam". As this is largely a black and white book of photographs I hope they convey some of this feeling.

Tony Butcher
Crawley Down, 2014

NEWHAVEN WEST QUAY BRANCH

A1X 32635 in Stroudley Livery as Brighton Works shunter, but with BR number, crosses the main road from the West Quay to Newhaven Shed past an aptly named pub. The bridge over from the West Quay had severe weight restrictions prohibiting all other classes from its use on this duty. (6.6.62)

A1X 32635 in Brighton Works livery crosses the swing road bridge from the West Quay Goods Yard at Newhaven to regain the main line station and shed. (6.6.62)

WESTERHAM BRANCH

H 31530 halts at the basic Chevening Halt on a Dunton Green to Westerham Branch local. Attempts to preserve the branch fell foul of the trackbed providing land for the building of the new M25. (8.10.61)

H Class 0-6-0 No.31530 approaches Westerham Station on the branch from Dunton Green only a couple of weeks before complete closure. (8.10.61)

SOUTH EASTERN SECTION OF THE SR

The complex junctions in the Petts Wood and Chislehurst area saw trains from Victoria or Charing Cross and Cannon Street changing over their routes to Dover and the east of Kent, as well as other services such as the Hasting trains with the flat sided stock. The wooded area, together with one or more winding main line connecting spurs, added to the pleasant rural nature of the setting in 1957. All these shots were taken in only a few hours one day, 15 April 1957. However, these junctions with the connecting spurs were all being re-laid and altered when visited again in 1958, and looked nothing like so attractive as before.

The down "Golden Arrow" headed by Britannia No.70014 "Iron Duke" in full regalia winds through the woods on the tortuous connecting spur from Bickley Junction onto the main line to Tonbridge and beyond at Orpington Junction.

Opposite: King Arthur Class No.30792 "Sir Hervis de Revel" runs through from St Mary Cray Junction with a Dover – Victoria train via Maidstone East. (15.4.57)

West Country No.34101 "Hartland" winds off the winding loop to gain the Tonbridge line with a Victoria – Dover Boat Train. (note the Pullmans in the consist).

Opposite: D1 Class 4-4-0 No.31735 joins the Victoria – Ramsgate main line after traversing the loop from Chislehurst with a van train to Dover and Folkestone via Chatham. (15.4.57)

Opposite: Large chimney Schools 30914 "Harrow" in immaculate black livery bustles past on the Chislehurst Loop with a Victoria – Dover train via Swanley.

Schools Class 30935 "Sevenoaks " passes Hither Green with a Charing Cross – Hastings train of flat sided stock needed for the tight tunnels on the line.

BB Class No.34072 "257 Squadron" gets a clear road south of Hither Green with the down afternoon "Man of Kent" (the 4.15pm from Charing Cross).

GREAT WESTERN MAIN LINE

On an ordinary day in the fifties on the Great Western main line from Paddington to the West Country a continual stream of Kings and Castles could be seen, usually in clean condition, on a succession of main line expresses and named trains with matching sets of smart chocolate and cream coaches in tow. A few County Class and the odd Hall also appeared on passenger, parcels and milk trains, as well as the 61XX Class 2-6-2 tanks on the local services to Slough, etc. Additionally a Cardiff Britannia normally worked the up and down "Red Dragon".

Opposite: Castle Class No.5023 "Brecon Castle" speeds away from Iver with the down "Capitals United Express". (24.4.57)

An immaculate 61XX 2-6-2T No.6167 shunts stock outside Paddington. At this time a brace of 61XX class operated all the local trains to Slough. (19.8.57)

King 4-6-0 No.6017 "King Edward IV" storms away from Iver on the 4.15 pm to Plymouth. (24.4.57)

Castle No.7023 speeds through Iver Station in charge of an up express. (24.4.57)

Castle 5049 "Earl of Plymouth" steams westwards near Iver with the down Kensington – Penzance milk train on 24 April 1957.

Castle No.5059 "Earl Cairns" (later to be preserved) appears from in its own exhaust near Iver with the up "Torbay Express" with all the stops out. (24.4.57)

THREE BRIDGES – EAST GRINSTEAD BRANCH

H Class 0-4-4 tanks were generally the standard motive power on the Three Bridges to East Grinstead Branch. An M7 or an E4 tank did occasionally appear, but I only saw one M7 working the line, as seen from the photographs below, and luckily a clean one at that. After 1962 the remaining H Class tanks and the odd M7 were gradually withdrawn from the line in 1963. Diesel multiple units then took over with the odd Standard Class 4 tank in the rush hours, before complete closure of the line in June 1965.

A nicely clean M7 Class 4-4-0 tank No.30055 runs downhill into Grange Road Station with the East Grinstead (High Level) – Three Bridges push and pull service on 16 March 1962.

At the next station on the line M7 30055 pulls away from Grange Road en route to the Brighton Line Junction at Three Bridges.

M7 30055 pauses at Rowfant, the only other station on the line. Note the gas lamps and ladders ready for use. The old station building seen here had been preserved under a preservation order and still stands somewhat derelict today. Early ideas of preserving a section of the line from Three Bridges to Rowfant never got off the ground. The sidings near Rowfant had housed a wartime fuel storage depot and was still in use at this time for other business purposes, which had probably encouraged the idea.

H Class 0-4-4T No.31551 storms up the bank out of Grange Road Station on a frosty morning in December 1961 with the Three Bridges – East Grinstead (High Level) push and pull. This in fact was the station for Crawley Down where I now live. The station and line are now all gone and houses built around but the track-bed still survives as the "Worth Way". The short line had three manually operated level crossings, one at Grange Road visible in the distance, one at Rowfant, and a third complete with crossing keeper house between Rowfant and Three Bridges. These would have been a big problem with modern day traffic. (17.12.61)

SECR tank No.31005 pauses at Rowfant with the East Grinstead – Three Bridges push and pull on an autumn day in 1961.

H Class 0-4-4T No.31551. The crewman hands the tablet to the signalman at the East Grinstead (High Level) Box while working the branch from Three Bridges. (28.1.62)

HAYLING ISLAND BRANCH

The Hayling Island Branch was the last haunt of the diminutive , but attractive A1X Class 0-6-0Ts (dating from the original A1 design of 1872 rebuilt in 1911) on passenger trains. The line closed to all normal traffic on Saturday 2 November 1963, there being no Sunday service. The very last train down the branch was the LCGB "Hayling Island Farewell" special, on the following day Sunday 3 November. The reason given for the line closure was the poor condition of the wooden bridge to the island seen in the picture on page 29. However it is unlikely it would have lasted much longer under the Beeching cuts regime.

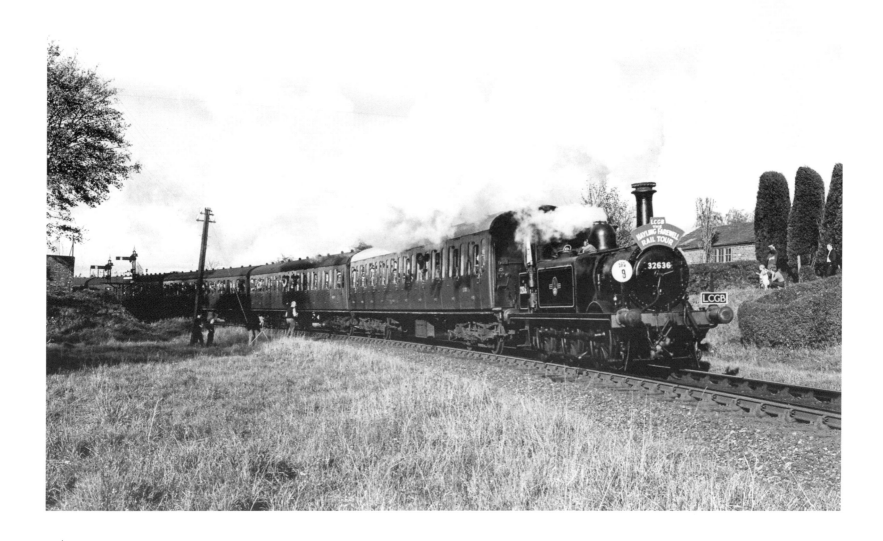

Watched by a considerable number of spectators, Q Class 0-6-0s Nos.30531 and 30543 pull away from Havant with the returning LCGB "Hayling Island Farewell Tour" en route to Chichester and then up the freight only truncated remains of the LBSC line to Midhurst Branch at Lavant in the late afternoon sunshine. The Qs demonstrate two different chimney types. The pilot engine has the large Lemaitre chimney fitted by Bulleid, while the train engine sports a standard BR chimney.

Opposite: A1X No.32636 pulls round the curve out of Havant on the Hayling Island Branch with the last day special on 3 November 1963 backed up in the rear by A1X 32670.

On a beautiful sunny November day immaculate A1X No.32636 approaches Langstone Halt banked at the rear by A1X No.32670 with the LCGB "Hayling Farewell" tour of 3/11/63. This was the last passenger train to Hayling Island before complete closure, and ended the use of the diminutive and classic A1X Class of 1870 origin on BR. The engines selected happened to be the first Stroudley Terriers built at Brighton Works in 1872 and the oldest steam locomotives working on BR.

A1X No.32646 Returns across the wooden bridge from Hayling Island a few days before line closure in November 1963.

A1X No.32646 rounds the bend out of Havant in normally rather dirty condition with a train to Hayling Island in October 1963, not long before complete closure of the branch.

KINGS ON SAUNDERTON BANK

By 1962 most of the still operational Kings were concentrated on the GWR Paddington-Birmingham-Wolverhampton main line. Thus one could still see a King as up or down express every hour, plus the odd Castle. I visited the line on the climb up Saunderton Bank from High Wycombe twice during this time. Most of the Kings still looked in good condition and were performing at speed. It is thus hard to believe that they were all withdrawn to scrap by the end of 1962, except for No.6018.

4-6-0 No.6021 "King Richard II" speeds down Saunderton Bank into West Wycombe with the up "Cambrian Coast Express" on 23 May 1962.

Opposite: King 6029 powers up the grade out of High Wycombe with a down express. It is hard to believe that these top engines running the Paddington to Birmingham and Wolverhampton service on an hourly basis in 1962 were all withdrawn by the end of the year, except for 6018 which was retained to the next April to run a last farewell special (see page 58). (23/5/62)

King Class No.6002 "King William IV" climbs past Bradenham village with the 2.10 am Paddington – Birkenhead. (18.8.62)

2-8-0 No.2855 making much ado of its load as it runs down the bank from Princess Risborough on a southbound freight, at the point where the up and down lines diverge at different levels. The down line passes through a tunnel, the up line does not. (18.8.62)

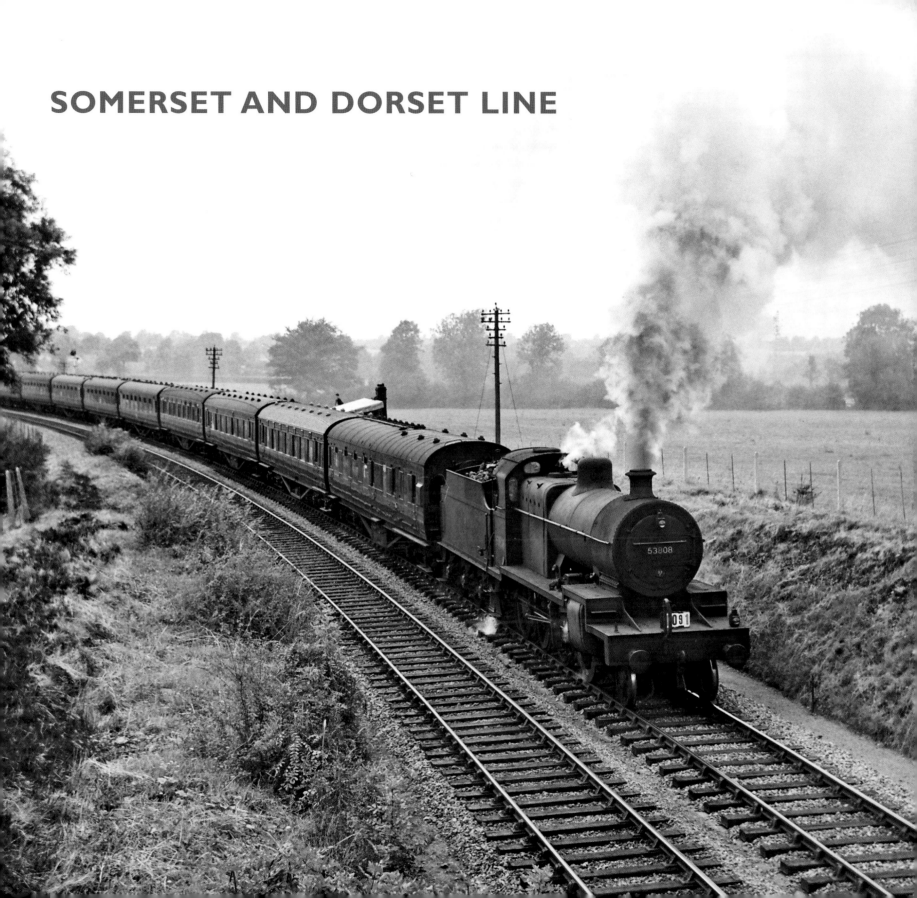

A dirty LMS 2P No.40697 pilots WC No.34041 "Dorchester" over the top of Masbury Summit, both steaming well on the SO 12.20 pm Bournemouth – Nottingham. This was the last year that the 2P Midland 4-4-0s were used regularly on piloting duty from Evercreech Junction. (29.7.61)

Previous page: SDJR 2-8-0 No.53808 climbs to Masbury Summit with the maximum unassisted load of 10 coaches for a '7F' with the SO through train, the 7.35 am from Nottingham. Most locomotives used on the the SDJR looked dirty and unkempt over the years. Although much beloved, the line was not called "The Slow and Dirty" for nothing. (29.7.61)

Very well turned out unrebuilt Bullied Light Pacifics Nos.34006 "Bude" and 34057 "Biggin Hill" pull away from
Evercreech Junction after a photostop with the returning LCGB "Somerset and Dorset Farewell" rail tour returning
from Bath Green Park to Bournemouth on the penultimate day before closure, 5 March 1966.

The gleaming unrebuilt West Countries Nos.34006 "Bude" and 34057 "Biggin Hill" side by side at Bath Green Park Shed having been turned for the return trip over the SDJR with the LCGB 'Farewell Special'. (5.3.66)

New power on the line – 9F 2-10-0 No.92000 climbs up to Chilcompton on the 0.35am Sheffield – Bournemouth (SO). (29.7.61)

Somerset and Dorset 7F 2-8-0, No.53808 (evidently given a special clean at Bath Green Park) halts at Shepton Mallet in the late afternoon sun with the LCGB "Somerset and Dorset" rail tour of 30/9/62 en route to Bath (Green Park), while traversing the whole length of the SDJR from Broadstone Junctiion. By this time 6 of this class of 11 had been withdrawn, but this engine was later preserved and is now in working order on the West Somerset Railway. This tour had an excellent itinerary, starting at Waterloo and traversing the Brockenhurst to Ringwood line in order to reach Broadstone behind a West Country Pacific. A trip was made up the Highbridge Branch behind Great Western 0-6-0, seen on the page overleaf. On arrival of the 2-8-0 at Bath a SDJR '4F' No.44558 took over to Bristol, where one of the last GWR 2-8-0 4700 Class No.4707 took over in the gloom to run back to London. Unfortunately the engine failed near Swindon, and a Hawksworth County Class engine had to be summoned to rescue the train

Immaculate unrebuilt West Country Class Pacifics Nos.34006 "Bude" and 34057 "Biggin Hill" wait in the pilot road at Evercreech Junction to head the LCGB "Farewell to the SDJR" tour to Bath before returning back over the Somerset and Dorset line on the last day of normal operation, 5 March 1966. Double headed Ivatt tanks had headed the special from Templecombe and up the branch to Highbridge before returning to Evercreech Junction. A Merchant Navy Pacific had initially brought the special from Waterloo to Templecombe, and finally returned the train from Bournemouth to London.

Opposite: Stanier '8F' 2-8-0 No.48309 prepares to leave Shepton Mallet with the first LCGB "Wessex Downsman" rail tour of 4 April 1965, and head south over the SDJR to Bournemouth West. This tour was so popular it was repeated a month later. By this time, towards the end of the line's life, 8Fs were quite common on the SDJR. Modified Hall No.6963 had brought the train to Bristol from Reading New Junction via Pewsey and Bradford-on-Avon after taking over from S15 No.30839, which had hauled the train from Waterloo via Ascot to Reading.

8F 2-8-0 No.48706 takes water at Evercreech Junction before proceding southwards with a Great Western Society special on the last day of normal operation on the SDJR before complete closure of the line north of Blanford Forum from 7 March 1966.

PADDINGTON DEPARTURES

Cardiff Canton Britannia Pacific No.70018 "Flying Dutchman" pulls out of Paddington with the "Red Dragon", the crack South Wales express to Cardiff. At this time this and "The Capitals United" were regular Britannia turns. (19.8.1957)

Immaculate Castle of Gloucester Shed pulls out of Paddington with the "Cheltenham Spa Express" on 19 August 1957, while on the left another Castle waits with the 5.05pm to Weston-Super-Mare.

Castle No.4096 "Highclere Castle" stands at the buffer stops in Paddington with a train from Cardiff and beyond. (24.4.57)

An unidentified King departs from Paddington with the 4.15 pm to Plymouth. By this time only two Kings were believed to still have the original single chimney. (19.8.57)

Classic Paddington departure King No. 6008, "King James II", makes an energetic departure with the 3.30 pm to Penzance some fifteen months earlier on the 8 March 1956

LAST SR ATLANTIC SPECIAL

Brighton Atlantic No.32424 "Beachy Head" stands in the shed yard at Newhaven beside Newhaven Town Station after heading the RCTS "Atlantic Farewell Special" from Victoria to Newhaven Harbour on Sunday 13 April 1958. The reason that particular route was chosen for the special run was to enact one of the Atlantic's normal working duties heading the Victoria – Newhaven boat trains. Other motive power on shed add to the add to the occassion were two A1Xs, and BR Std. C1.4 No.80154 (the last locomotive built at Brighton). A Ramsgate-based Schools No.30910 "Merchant Taylors" was also resident in the shed. The BR 2-6-4T then hauled the special on the Newhaven (Town) to Brighton leg. Enthusiasts on the Bluebell Railway are nowadays building a replica of a Brighton Atlantic which just goes to reinforce the notion that an opportunity was certainly missed in 1958 to secure the last of the Atlantic Class engines.

Later in the day the H2 Class Brighton Atlantic "Beachy Head" backs down onto Brighton Shed for the last time after hauling the RCTS Farewell Special, having run light engine from Newhaven. The locomotive was by then the last operational Atlantic on British Railways. The other last five Atlantics had all been withdrawn during August and October in 1956, leaving "Beachy Head" to soldier on by itself. "Beachy Head" was condemned and scrapped soon afterwards. What a pity it could not have been preserved at the time.

Opposite: On that same Sunday, at the shed the two very well turned out A1X 0-6-0Ts Nos.32636 and 32640, stood on the spur to the Railway wharf, alongside the 60ft turntable. They pose with the celebrity Atlantic, whilst their respective crews and enthusiasts alike inspect and admire them all. Only No.32640 was actually involved with the special, as it had hauled the seven coach train away from Harbour Station and up to Newhaven (Town) Station. Note that both of the tank engines have different coal bunkers; No.32636 has a slightly taller bunker – with just inches in it – whilst No.32640 has a longer bunker.

Bird's eye view of Brighton engine shed on that memorable day in April 1958 with No.32424 "Beachy Head" in the foreground. Being a Sunday the shed was packed full of largely clean engines. Brighton Shed had always hosted a wealth of SR types and on this particular day it still presented an excellent selection of locomotives. In view are: C2X, E4, K, L, M7, Urie S15, WC/BB, and BR Std. Two preserved engines were in addition brought out on display, the Adams 4-4-0 and A1X 0-6-0T "Boxhill". Blowing off in the middle distance can be seen King Arthur No.36796 "Sir Dodinas le Savage" which was waiting to haul the special back to London via the Brighton Line. The special consisted of seven carriages including a Pullman Buffet car. In the far distance, on the viaduct, a diminutive A1X can just be seen returning from the morning session at Newhaven Shed.

D CLASS LAST YEAR ON REDHILL – DORKING LINE

A member of a fast disappearing Class 'D' No.31577 of Wainright SEC 1901 design heads away from Dorking with a birdcage set on a misty morning on the 1.22 pm to Guildford. (4.1.56)

'Contre Jour' shot of old stager 'D' Class 31488 with birdcage set steams out from Dorking en route to Guildford. (31.12.55)

'D' Class 4-4-0 No.31488 works out her last days on the Redhill – Reading line, shedded at Guildford. Here seen with a SECR birdcage set entering Gomshall with a train from Redhill on 29 December 1955. It looks as if the station porter is also about to take a photograph of this old stager and is hurrying along the platform opposite with his camera.

Opposite: A nicely clean 'D' Class No.31549 for this date, complete with birdcage set, runs along under the lee of Boxhill with the 10.51 am Guildford to Redhill on 16 April 1956. This was the last year of the 'D's on regular service trains.

BANBURY STATION

Modified Hall No.7906 "Fron Hall" makes a fine exhaust as it enters Banbury with a down stopping train. (9.3.56)

Unmodified King No.6005 "King George II" steams into Banbury with a Birmingham & Wolverhampton Express. (9.3.56)

EXETER STATION AND SHEDS

The down (westbound) "Cornishman" enters Exeter St David's behind Castle 7029 "Clun Castle" on 28 August 1957 before modification and preservation! Note the entry from north end of the station in contrast to the SR trains going west travelling in the opposite direction.

King 4-6-0 No.6021 "King Richard II" coasts across the layout into Exeter St David's from the south with the up "Cornish Riviera Ltd". (28.8.57)

On the same day a stone train probably from Meldon Quarry waits in the central road at Exeter St David's with a 700 Class 0-6-0 at one end and a Mogul at the other awaiting further assistance to surmount the climb into Exeter Central.

One of the three Adams tanks of 1882 vintage retained for working the Lyme Regis Branch, 0415 Class 4-4-2 tank No.30582, sits in the sunshine outside Exmouth Junction Shed, waiting to return to Axminster for further work on the branch on 28 March 1957. Assuming that two engines were working the branch during this busy holiday period, the tank would not be going until Saturday (changeover day) for its next week-long stint on the branch. Whichever member of the trio returned to Exmouth Junction for its washout, a spare was always available to cover failures. The tank was built by Robert Stephenson & Co. and entered traffic in 1885. To its left is clean looking Merchant Navy No.35009 "Shaw Savill".

Opposite: N Class No.31840 blasts away up the 1-37 bank from Exeter St David's to Exeter Central with a freight piloted by E1/R 0-6-2T No.32124, when E1/Rs were still in use for assistance up the bank. (28.8.57)

GWR SPECIALS

The last operational King 6018 "King Henry VI" halts at Southall Station with the SLS Farewell special from Birmingham. This King had been kept back in operational condition to haul this last special on 28 April 1963.

14XX 1420 and 0-6-0T 6435 pull forward under the road bridge at St Phillips Marsh Shed after heading a special from Worcester to Gloucester South Junction. 6435 then piloted 7029 "Clun Castle" to Bristol while 1420 made its way light to there. By then all three engines were preserved and owned by Pat Whitehouse. The special was used to transfer the tanks to the South Devon Railway at Buckfastleigh. (17.10.65)

14XX Class 1444 departs from the branch terminus at Calne with a GWPS afternoon special on 20 September 1964. The tour had started at Swindon and heads for the mainline at Westbury after traversing the branch. By this time there were few 14XX Class remaining. The only passenger service left for their use being the Gloucester and Chalford push and pull.

Castle Class No.7029 "Clun Castle" basks in the late afternoon sun at Chester (LNWR)
Shed before returning to London with the second of the Ian Allan Specials "The Zulu",
commemorating the farewell to the Great Western Paddington to Birkenhead route on 4/3/67.

Preserved Castle No.7029 climbs the 1 in 86 gradient up past Llangollen Junction with the first of the SLS specials from Birmingham to Chester commemorating the GWR route to Birkenhead, on the second day these specials were run on the 5 March 1967. The second special that day was headed by Black Five No.44680, thus with no reappearance of 4079.

Preserved Castle No.4079 "Pendennis Castle" in immaculate restored condition storms away from Chester near Pulford. It is en route back to Birmingham in readiness to attack the formidable Gresford Bank at a gradient of 82 to 1 for 3½ miles with the first of the returning Ian Allan specials commemorating the Birkenhead GW route from Paddington on 4/3/67 – this train was named the "Birkenhead Flyer". This was to be the last outing by 4079 before it was sold (rather strangely) to a mineral railway in Australia, but has since been repatriated, and is now being restored to working order once more.

Opposite: Now in preserved form Castle Class, No.7029 "Clun Castle" speeds southwards through Rossett at the foot of Gresford Bank with the second of the returning Ian Allan Birkenhead route farewell specials from Chester to Birmingham (named "The Zulu") on 4/3/67, in the last of the afternoon light.

LSWR MAIN LINE

A favourite spot of mine when I started railway photography was Surbiton, and many of my earliest Southern pictures were taken here. In one day it was possible to see almost the whole Lord Nelson Class, less the odd one in the Works, etc.

A well groomed Lord Nelson No.30861 "Lord Anson" blasts through Surbiton with an afternoon Bournemouth Express. (22.3.57)

A Class N No.31634 picks up speed through Raynes Park on a presumed Basingstoke semi-fast. However this is an unusual duty for this class and the head code is wrong for the Waterloo line. A well-turned-out young lady watches the photographer and not the train. (8/8/57)

Rebuilt Merchant Navy No.35010 "Blue Star" speeds through Surbiton on a sunny spring afternoon with the down "Royal Wessex". (22.3.57)

Earliest of the H15 4-6-0 Class designed by Urie in 1914 No.30482 speeds through Surbiton bound for Southhampton Terminus. To judge from the schoolboys on the platform, school is already over at Surbiton County for the afternoon. These oldest LSWR machines were nicknamed "Chonkers". (22.3.57)

MN No.35017 charges through Earlsfield Station with a down express. (1.4.58)

Opposite: Lord Nelson Class No.30854 "Howard of Effingham" speeds through Raynes Park on a down Bournemouth Express, but the ganger with his basket hardly looks up as it thunders past him on the near line on 8 August 1957.

"The Boys of the Old Brigade" N15 No.30452 "Sir Melingrance" starts the 2.54 pm to Southampton Terminus out of Waterloo while an old LSWR Electric stands in the adjoining platform on the 1 April, 1958.

On the same day a King Arthur enters Waterloo on an express from Plymouth while WC 34011 "Tavistock" waits to depart on another West Country Express.

Opposite: King 6029 swings through the promenade at Dawlish, with the beaches well occupied, on a high summer day in '57 with the down "Cornish Riviera Ltd". (27.8.57)

SOUTH DEVON GWR COASTAL LINE

In 1957 I spent a holiday staying at Dawlish for two weeks. The procession of trains and locomotives along the coast here would now be hard to imagine. Although not having my own transport at this time it was fairly easy to access the Exeter – Plymouth line by train and the odd bus.

Grange Class No.6846 "Ruckley Grange" steams out onto the sea wall at Teignmouth with an eastbound freight. (5.9.57)

Castle No.5053 "Earl Cairns" skirts the sea wall near Teignmouth with the 4-5 pm Exeter – Plymouth. (30.8.57)

41XX Praire No.4174 rounds the curve at Dawlish Warren with an Exeter – Newton Abbot local. (25.8.57)

Castle No.5093 "Upton Castle" speeds out from Parson and Cark tunnel onto the
sea wall between Dawlish and Teignmouth; passing time 5 p.m. approx. (30.8.57)

SUSSEX SPECIALS

34066 "Spitfire" storms up the bank past Rotherfield and Marks Cross Station on the 'Cukoo' Line en route from Tunbridge Wells West to Pevensey with the LCGB /RCTS "Sussex Downsman" of 22 March 1964. Here N Class 31411 took over to Lewes (East Sidings) and afterwards after reversal to Brighton.

Although the Q1s were regarded as the 'ugly duckling's of the Southern, several appeared on rail tours in the latter years. By the time of the LCGB "Wealdsman" tour, the Q1 class was down to only six survivors, which were employed on various freight and ballast duties. Q1 No.33006 had been employed on an REC special over the Horsham – Guildford line on the day before, which was the last day of normal operation, the next day being Sunday had no scheduled service. Q1s Nos.33006 and 33027 were booked to head the last stage of the tour from Horsham to Guildford and then to Waterloo via Cobham. Here they are seen leaving Baynards Station after a photo stop in the evening sun with the "Wealdsman", being viewed by a quite large crowd of local spectators come to see the very last train over the line. In fact this tour also marked the closures of the East Grinstead to Three Bridges and Tunbridge Wells West via Forest Row lines, as well as most of the Cuckoo Line to Eastbourne, with the elimination of steam services on all these lines.

SR Moguls Nos.N 31411 and U 31803 speed round the curve into Cooksbridge with the returning LCGB "Wealdsman" rail tour en route to Haywards Heath from Eastbourne, via Lewes and Keymer Junction. A grubby U Class 2-6-0, No.31803 had already double headed the "Wealdsman" up the climb through Rotherfield and Mark Cross with clean N Class 2-6-0 No.31411, en route to Eastbourne with the last train to travel over the entire length of the 'Cuckoo Line' before partial closure on 13/6/65. However, the dirty U was an unfortunate last minute replacement for a failed clean locomotive and had been the front piloting engine until it reached Eastbourne, having already traversed the Three Bridges – East Grinstead Branch and the line through Forest Row to Groombridge Junction behind the engines with this arrangement. At the remains of Eastbourne Shed for servicing the locomotives had thankfully been reversed in order, hence this particular shot. All traffic was withdrawn on the Cuckoo Line as far south as Hailsham, but the line to Polegate stayed open another three years.

Looking very smart LSWR Class M7 0-4-4T, No.30055 and the preserved T9 No.120, stand at Rotherfield and Mark Cross in the evening sun. The M7 had been detached from the train engine, having piloted the LCGB "Sussex Coast Ltd" rail tour of 24 June 1962 from Eastbourne over the Cuckoo Line up the climb though Mayfield. The T9 then proceeded to London Bridge via East Grinstead and Oxted. By this time only 19 of the once ubiquitous M7 Class survived.

On arrival of the LCGB "Midhurst Belle" rail tour from Guildford behind USA 0-6-0T No.30064, immaculate Q Class 0-6-0 No.30530 backs the train out of the Guildford line platform at Christ's Hospital before heading down the Horsham-Arundel main line to Hardnam Junction to take the train over the freight only branch to Midhurst. This was the final passenger working over the branch before its closure to all traffic from 10 May 1966. 30530 was one of the last Q class in operation and was one of seven of the class fitted with a BR chimney and one given an ugly stovepipe chimney in 1953, which superseded the Lemetaire multiple-jet blastpipe chimneys fitted by Bulleid to the twenty strong class which were only partly sucessful. The locomotive was withdrawn in December 1964, ending its days as shed pilot at Nine Elms. Although seven Qs officially survived at this time, some were stored and others kept for snow plough duties in the winter months at Redhill, Guildford, Salisbury, and Eastleigh.

Opposite: The unrelenting withdrawal of SR steam locomotives during the mid 1960s meant that the variety of classes was rapidly shrinking and consequently the small fleet of USA tanks suddenly found favour with railtour organisers. Here USA 0-6-0T No.30064, in BR lined green livery and now the shed pilot at Guildford, prepares to depart from Baynards Station after a photostop with the RCTS/LCGB "Midhurst Belle" rail tour of 18 October 1964, en route to Christ's Hospital and an engine change. Fourteen locomotives of this class were acquired in 1946 from the USA Army Transportation Corp. chiefly to replace the ageing ex-LSWR B4 0-4-0 Ts for working in Southampton Docks. Six examples were painted in lined green during 1963/1964 and several have survived into preservation at the Bluebell, Kent and East Sussex, and Keighley and Worth Valley Railways.

Immaculate ex-LBSCR E4 Class No.32503 takes over the LCGB "Sussex Coast Ltd" rail tour at Horsham from preserved T9 4-4-0 No.120 together with E6 Class 0-6-2T No.32617, before visiting the freight only Midhurst Branch on 24/6/62. The E4 Class was the most numerous of R.J. Billington's 0-6-2T classes of which 75 were built at Brighton Works between 1897 and 1902. Largely confined to the Southern Central Section only 10 survived by this date; 5 at Brighton, 4 at Nine Elms, and 1 at Eastleigh. Fortunately one of the class is preserved at the Blubell Railway – No.32473.

CENTRAL SECTION OF SOUTHERN

Collision imminent! Well, not really. H No.31005 moves down the shed yard and passes sister No.31518 at right angles on the turntable in this 1 June 1962 view. By 1956 seven of these 0-4-0Ts were allocated to Tunbridge Wells West, shedcode 73F. The depot had a pleasant country background. The line is now running as the Spa Valley preserved railway as far as Groombridge Junction, and retains the engine shed, but the once impressive station has been cut back to a single platform alongside the shed.

H Class No.31005 halts at Ashurst with the Oxted – Tunbridge Wells West push and pull. Note the gas lamps and the old lady also in June 1962.

Class 4 75069 makes a spirited departure from Tunbridge Wells West while a Mogul stands outside the shed on the left, with a train to Victoria via Hever and Oxted. (1.6.62)

CAMBRIAN LINES

BR 2-6-2T No.82009 starts a southbound freight out of Towyn yard. (26.6.62)

GWR 2-6-0 No.6339 crosses the estuary from Barmouth into Morfa Mawddock (late of Barmouth Junction) with the 12.45 pm from Pwllheli to Birkenhead. (29.6.62)

2-6-0 No.75020 in green lining waits at Machynalleth in readiness to head the 6.55 pm to Porthmadog. (28.6.62)

2-6-0 No.6339 enters Dollgelly Station with the 7.50 am from Pwellhei to Birkenhead. (29.6.62)

PLYMOUTH AND CORNWALL

Nicely clean Beattie well tank No.30587 crosses the main road at Dunmere Halt
with the returning Wenford Bridge Branch – Wadebridge Goods. (29.3.61)

Beattie well tank No.30586, the one with the square splashers in the yard outside Wadebridge Shed with the shunter and his pole in evidence on 29 March 1961.

Beattie well tank No.30587 approaches the main Bodmin – Wadebridge road with the daily freight from Wanford Bridge. (30.3.61)

Castle 4-6-0 No.4088 "Dartmouth Castle" enters Plymouth North Road Station with
the up "Cornishman" having traversed the curving viaduct on the right. (27.8.57).

On Thursday 29 August 1957 West Country, No. 34021 "Dartmoor" heads a freight bound for Exeter past the southern boundary of Friary Shed with one of its Ivatt tanks standing in the shed approach. Which route the freight train took is unknown, but SR enginemen often worked over the WR mainline via Newton Abbot to keep route knowledge up-to-date in case of any possible diversions, which it might be added were not infrequent. It was not unusual to see the Pacifics hauling freight over the route between Plymouth and Exeter via Okehampton, as Friary had no other suitable motive power, and tender engines, such as Mogul 2-6-0s, were not always available, from Exmouth Junction or elsewhere.

A smart looking Ivatt 2-6-2T No. 41316 stands out the front of Plymouth Friary Shed on the 27 August 1957, only recently transferred from the South Eastern Section to judge from its 74A Ashford headcode still in place. Up to four Ivatt tanks were finally transferred to Friary to take over the duties of older engines being withdrawn, including O2 and B4 tanks.

45XX tank No. 4564 runs round at St. Ives with the branch train on 30 March 1961.

Immaculate King No.6002 "King William IV" backs out from Plymouth Laira Shed to take out the up "Cornish Riviera Express". (29.8.57)

HEMYOCK BRANCH

4XX 0-4-2T No.1471 departs from Tiverton Junction with the 1.42 pm to Hemyock with a single ex-Barry coach on 17 September 1962.

The 1.42 pm from Tiverton arrives at the charming terminus of Hemyock behind 14XX 1471 and its single old Barry coach. (17.9.62)

Opposite: Following their withdrawal and replacement by ex-GWR 1366 0-6-0 Class Pannier tanks in August 1962 from the mineral line between Wadebridge and Wenford Bridge used for china clay traffic, two of the three surviving Beattie 2-4-0 well tanks of 1874/75 vintage were brought up to London after withdrawal from storage at Eastleigh Shed to work two glorious commemorative rail tours from Waterloo to Hampton Court and Shepperton. Here Beattie tanks Nos.30585 and 30587 are seen about to leave Surbiton on the outward run to Hampton Court with the first tour, the RCTS/SLS "South Western Suburban Tour" which took place in fine winter weather on 2/12/62. (Note the porter taking a photograph). At Hampton Court the tanks nearly had to drop their fires due to lack of water, and had to be rescued in the nick of time by the local Fire Brigade. The three Beattie well tanks survived so long at Wadebridge principally to haul the china clay trains on the Wenford Bridge Branch due to weight restrictions and tight curves, and outlasted their sister engines by some 63 years. Both engines were thankfully preserved and have now been restored to working order in BR black livery at the Flour Mill Works in the Forest of Dean for the Bodmin and Wenford Railway and at the Buckingham Railway Centre at Quainton Road. The GWR 1366 0-6-0 Pannier tanks took over working the branch for a further two years, reportedly being the last active BR steam in Cornwall.

BEATTIE WELL TANKS FAREWELL

The last survivor of the H16 4-6-2T Class was also used on these Beattie farewell runs for the middle leg of the special from Wimbledon Yard to Chessington North and return. 301517 had also been retained specially from the scrap yard for these specials. Here in less pleasant weather than for the first Beattie well tanks farewell tour, H16 No.30517 4-6-2T climbs up to New Malden on the Chessington Branch on 26 December 1962.

Beattie 0-4-2 well tanks Nos.30585 and 30587 pull away from Surbiton, gleaming in the winter sun, with the first leg of their farwell swansong runs on 2 December 1962 heading initially for Hampton Court.

BASINGSTOKE AREA

All photographs in this section were taken on the same day, 17 April 1957.

Already an old stager N15 30751 "Elaine" built by Urie in 1918 and modified by him in 1928, trundles towards Basingstoke with a small pick-up freight on the slow line, not many months before its withdrawal. (17.4.57)

Opposite: Unrebuilt MN 35030 "Elder Dempster Line" in almost original condition enters Basingstoke past the shed with an up Bournemouth Express. Note the school boys train spotting on the bank by the shed. No health and safety issue in those days! (17.4.57)

LN Class No.30857 "Lord Howe" approaches Basingstoke with a Bournemouth Express on the fast line and may not stop at Basingstoke. (17.4.57)

On 17 April 1957, one of the oldest surviving Urie King Arthurs – and in fact the last of the class with Bulleid multiple jet blast pipe and large diameter chimney – No.30755 "The Red Knight" is stabled by the old coaling stage at Basingstoke. The locomotive had just days left before it was called into works and condemned. Basingstoke had a number of these old 4-6-0s allocated, including No.30755 seen here; all followed to the scrapheap during that summer of 1957 leaving only No.30758 operational until the following February.

Opposite: Looking in smart condition for its age N15 No.30455 "Sir Launcelot" of original Maunsell design of 1925 steams away from Basingstoke Station with a semi-fast to Waterloo. (17.4.57)

Double chimney BR Class 4 No.75075 in clean condition on the turntable at Basingstoke Shed ready for a westbound train. In the right background can be seen the back corridor tender of a special engine, namely A3 preserved pacific "Flying Scotsman". 4472 had worked down from London with the then annual "Farnborough Flyer" on 10 September 1966. Note the clean white overalls of the crew for the celebrated visitor. Anoher five of these Standard Class 4 engines were allocated to Basingstoke from 1956 onwards fitted with the larger BR 4725 gallon tender, as the SR had no water troughs. Typical duties included semi-fasts to Salisbury and Waterloo, as well as the Portsmouth to Cardiff and Brighton to Plymouth workings.

SOUTH DEVON – KINGSWEAR LINE

Castle No.7000 "Viscount Portal" puts on the brakes as it enters Churston with the up Torbay Express. (2.9.57)

Castle 5091 "Cleeve Abbey" climbs up to Churston with the Kingswear portion of the up "Cornishman". Note the full chocolate and cream stock. (2.9.57)

Opposite: Castle 5092 "Tresco Abbey" steams down to Greenway Tunnel from Churston with the down Torbay Express. (2.9.57)

SR PRINCIPAL SHEDS
Stewarts Lane

Very well turned out Britannia No.70014 "Iron Duke" with full regalia prepares to back out of Stewart's Lane shed to head the "Golden Arrow" out of Victoria on 1 April 1958. 70014 was one of two Britannias sent to Sewart's Lane in September 1951 to head this prestigious and heavy Pullman train, the other being No.70004 "William Shakespeare". In the steam age the boat trains linking Britain with the continent were much more important to international travel than these days and the Pullman stock "Golden Arrow" was probably the most important working on the SR.

BB Class 4-6-2 No.34084 "253 Squadron" is stabled beside the steam crane at Stewart's Lane beneath the bridge which carries the line from Factory Junction to Longehedge Junction over the shed yard on 1 April 1958. Not every shed had a crane, but some were maintained at strategic points for emergencies.

On a misty morning LI Class 4-4-0 No.31753 stands in front of the coaling stage at Stewart's Lane having just come off the Night Ferry double heading with a West Country behind. The overnight working was very heavy with the French Wagons-lit sleeping coaches and required double heading throughout, hence the supplied 4-4-0 from Dover Shed. (1.11.56)

Eastleigh

A quite clean rebuilt Westcountry No.34025 "Whimple" takes water at Eastleigh on 14 October 1961. The Pacific was a fairly recent acquisition for 71A having been transferred from Bricklayers Arms at the end of the previous May. 34025 was the fifth of the class to be rebuilt and emerged from Eastleigh on 26 October 1957. The Lord Nelson behind does not look so smart, as it must by then nearing the end of its days.

Drummond T9 Class 4-4-0 No.30707 of 1899 vintage stands outside its home shed of Eastleigh on a sunny evening, looking relatively clean. On this Wednesday of April 1956, the need for a 15 road engine shed housing 120 plus engines does not seem to be justified.

Adams 0395 0-6-0 Class No.30566 introduced in 1885 still survives as a shunter in Eastleigh Works Yard, April 1958. By then it must have been one of the last working members of this very old class.

The last surviving S15, No.30837, taking water at Eastleigh Shed on the occasion of the "S15 Commemorative Rail Tour" on 9 January 1966 which was organised by the Locomotive Club of Great Britain. The nicely turned out 4-6-0 had been withdrawn during the previous September along with the other remaining four members of the class, but retained in operational condition for this last special from Waterloo to Eastleigh via Alton and the Mid-Hants Line and return. The special was in fact repeated a week later, but this time in the snow! After the event No.30837 was put back into store and unfortunately scrapped. Ironically seven other scrapped members of the class eventually found their way into preservation, but not this immaculate one.

Nine Elms Shed

LSWR Urie original design of H15 No.30482 looking relatively clean over the ashpits at Nine Elms Shed in company with a Battle of Britain 4-6-2. (1.4.58)

KESR FAREWELL

The last surviving SECR O1 Class 0-6-0 No.31065 pilots Class C No.31592 up the bank to Horsmonden Tunnel while traversing the Hawkhurst Branch with the LCGB "South Eastern Ltd" on 11 June 1961. The branch closed to normal traffic the next day.

Opposite: A representative line up of locomotives at Nine Elms Old Shed at this date of 1 April 1958. A full row of engines comprising M7, SR Mogul, Lord Nelson, 73116, E4, and a West Country are on view. The Old Shed had 15 roads and here are seen almost half of these.

H Class 31308 and D1 4-4-0 No.31749 enters Robertsbridge with the LCGB Special of 11 June 1961 in readiness for handing over to the A1X to take the last train up the KESR before complete closure. These two engines headed the special from Paddock Wood, having taken over from the same D1 and an L1, which had preceded them to Paddock Wood over the Maidstone West Branch via Lewisham and Strood from Victoria.

Late in the day A1X 32662 with A1X 32670 at the rear steam into Bodiam past the hop fields on the last special over the KESR line with the LCGB "The South Eastern Ltd".

Immaculate A1X 0-6-0Ts Nos 32662 and 32670 take water at Robertsbridge in preparation for heading the LCGB special up the KESR line.

SUMMER SATURDAYS ON SOUTH DEVON BANKS

On a summer sunny Saturday in the late 1950s I spent possibly the best day's photography of my life on the South Devon line from Totnes up the climb to the top of Rattery Bank and over the summit. On that day 7 September 1957 there was an endless succession of double-headed expresses from both directions using almost every possible combination of GWR 4-6-0s. I only saw one train with a single engine, that being a Hall with a shorter stopping train. I also photographed on another summer Saturday and saw double-headed Kings again, but the weather was unfortunately cloudy and dull. All the photographs below except one were taken on the 7 September.

Castle No.4075 "Cardiff Castle" is piloted up the 1 in 57 climb up Rattery Bank past Tigley Box on 7 September 1957 by Manor No.7814 "Fringford Manor". The climb of Rattery Bank westbound starts almost directly out of Totnes at 1 in 60 to 52 and only slackens a little to 1 in 90 to 95 in the last part of the 4 mile climb to the summit tunnel.

Opposite: Hall No.6940 "Didlington Hall" piloted by an equally immaculate Grange halts at Brent before continuing westwards to Plymouth.

Manor 7813 "Freshford Manor" and Castle 5021 "Whittington Castle" surmount the steepest part of Rattery Bank with a down Saturday express.

Super Power! Kings Nos.6004 "King George III" and 6021"King Richard II" attack the 1-52 of Rattery Bank with Saturdays Only relief to the "Cornish Riviera Ltd". The pilot engine had been detached from the "Cornish Riviera Ltd" at Newton Abbot as it did not stop at Plymouth on summer Saturdays and then piloted the following relief to Plymouth.

A pair of Halls commence the climb of Rattery Bank out of Totnes to the west.

Castle No.4096 "Highclere Castle" piloted by a Hall sweep down Rattery Bank as Manor 7820 "Dinmore Manor" pilots another Castle 5092 "Truro Abbey" up past Tigley Box on the down "Cornish Riviera Ltd". The up train is the "Cornishman".

Opposite: Castle Class 7031 "Cromwell's Castle" struggles up the last steepest part of Dainton Bank in the eastbound direction to the summit tunnel with the maximum unassisted load of 10 coaches on a dull weather day, 26 August 1957. The climb of Dainton Bank from the west is almost as steep and onerous as in the down direction, namely 1in 76 to 1 in 37 at the top for 2 miles.

REDHILL – READING LINE

The second main place I took my first photographs (after Surbiton already referred to) was the Redhill to Guildford Section of the line to Reading. The line was relatively near to my family home and later to my own house, and was also near my work in my earlier years. As well as being a country and scenic line, it ran a full steam-hauled service for both passenger and freight before the withdrawal of all steam-hauled services on 3 January 1965. I did not have my own transport until 1960 so in earlier years visits were made by train and then walking along the North Downs where several footpaths led down the hillside to foot level crossings, which was very pleasant enough in good weather. I favoured the climb out of Dorking to Gomshall summit, and I was lucky to just be in time to see the last of the lovely old D Class 4-4-0s working on this line in 1956, by which time I had my first reasonable camera. (See section starting p49)

A double-headed local with SR Moguls U Class No.31628 and N class No.31831, climbing up between Deepdene and Dorking Town in April 1964. U 31628, although looking recently ex-works had to be removed at Dorking Town owing to a shed coupling link. Double-headed workings on the line were very rare, and probably only occurred at odd times to transfer an otherwise light engine back along the line.

Opposite: S15 Class 30837 powers up the bank from Dorking with a heavy westbound freight to Guildford and beyond destined to be the last survivor of its class on 31 December 1955.

Manor Class No.7809 "Cookham Manor" departs from Betchworth with
the morning GWR turn from Redhill to Reading in September 1962.

GW Mogul 5368 puts on a good turn of speed as it pulls away up grade from Dorking on the climb to Gomshall with the single GW morning working to Reading. (31.12.55)

BR Standard Class 4 2-6-0, No.76062 storms up the bank out of Dorking at almost the same spot as in the previous picture with a Saturdays Only through train from Margate to Wolverhampton. (4.2.56)

Immaculately turned out by Redhill Shed N Class 2-6-0 No.31411 speeds away from Redhill on the Tonbridge line in the last of the afternoon light, with the LCGB "Maunsell Commemorative" rail tour of 3/1/65, marking the complete elimination of steam on the Southern Central Section between Reading-Redhill, and Redhill-Tonbridge. The engine headed this final leg of the special back to London via the Crowhurst spur in the gathering gloom to return via the East Grinstead and Oxted line to East Croydon and Victoria. The Redhill-Reading line was very much a last stronghold of the Maunsell Moguls on passenger work.

A nicely clean N No.31411 again tops Gomshall Bank and runs over the summit en route to Redhill. This engine became one of the last operational SR Moguls, and was used on a number of specials. (25.4.62)

Earliest of the U Class rebuilt from K Class 2-6-4 "River" tanks, No. 31790 climbs up from Deepdene to Dorking Town in the snow on 28 December 1964 only a few days before the withdrawal of all steam on the route on 3 January 1965.

'N' Class 31816 enters Gromshall and Shere Station from Redhill and Dorking with snow on the ground on 28 December 1964, again only just before the end of steam on the route to Reading, as might be in keeping with its very dirty unkempt state.

ISLE OF WIGHT

W31 "Chale" emerges from the tunnel though St Boniface Town into Ventnor Station with its train on 4 September 1965.

W24 "Calbourne" exchanges the tablet at Smallbrook Junction with a Ventnor – Ryde train in September 1963.

The fireman of W27 cleans out the smokebox at Ventnor. (August 1963)

O2 Class O-4-4T No.W18 "Ringwood" rounds the curve away from
Ryde St Johns, seen in the distance, with a Ventnor line train. (4.9.65)

On a fine summer day O2 No.W26 "Whitwell" departs from Ryde
Pierhead alongside the pier tramway with a Cowes-bound train.
Note the ferry steamers in the background at sea. (September 1963)

IOW O2 No.W14 "Fishbourne" rounds the curve at Smallbrook Junction with a freight for the Cowes line. (September 1963)

O2 W24 "Calbourne" leaves Ryde Pier Head Station with a train to Ventnor with the Electric Tramway in the foreground. (September 1963)

Opposite: IOW W27 "Merstone" arrives at Ventnor terminus with a train from Ryde and is about to take water. Note the rather precariously poised phone box. (4.9.65)

SR SPECIALS

Two of the last active Maunsell Moguls U No.31791 and N 31630 depart from Windsor and Eton Riverside in the evening light to head the second of the RTCS "Longmoor Specials" of 30 June 1966 back to London. Both were withdrawn in June 1966 with two other survivors.

Opposite: A2 60532 "Blue Peter" makes a fine sight as it winds its train onto the slow line through Surbiton with the LCGB A2 "Commemorative Rail Tour" to Exeter. Unfortunately the A2 stalled on Honiton Bank and only got back to Westbury, where a Britannia was due to take over for the run back to London, hours late.

SR 'USA' Class 0-6-0Ts 30064 and 30073 both in BR lined green livery run down the the branch to Fawley in a sylvan setting near Marchwood with the "Solent Tour" of 20/3/66 organised by the RCTS. Both engines were shunters at Eastleigh Works and Shed by this time. This tour started from Waterloo behind Battle of Britain 34090 "602 Squadron" to Salisbury. Standard Class 4 No.75070 then hauled the train to Southampton Ocean Terminal, where two USAs took over to Fawley, before 75070 hauled the train again to Fareham. Here U 31639 took over for a short trip down the freight only Gosport Branch, before both engines then double-headed the special back to Waterloo.

Opposite: The only known visit of an "A3" to the SR to haul a special was 60112 "St Simon" on 25 August 1963 (except for 4472 in preservation). Here 60112 waits to depart from Waterloo to Hamworthy achieving a reportedly 100mph down Micheldever Bank.

In wintry conditions from a previous day's snowfall, strangers to the area, SR Mogul No.31639 piloting Q1 0-6-0 No.33006, prepare to leave Stratford Old Town Station, having travelled the SMJR Joint line from Fenny Compton with the HCRS "Six Counties" special of 7 March 1965. By now the SMJR was a freight only line and would be closed to all traffic later in 1965. The train then continued to Wellingborough Shed where both engines were serviced after reversing onto the LMS lines at Leamington Spa and proceeding via Rugby and Northampton. The train returned to London Paddington via a circuitous route through Bedford, Oxford and Thame.

Feltham Shed, Maunsell S15, 4-6-0, No.30837 departs from New Alresford for Eastleigh with the LCGB "S15 Commemorative Rail Tour" of 9/1/66. This was certainly to be the last run of an S15 class as the engine had been specially retained for this last special, having been officially withdrawn in September 1965. In fact the tour was repeated a week later but in the snow, so that the train was double headed with No.31639 over the 'Little Alps' to Eastleigh (see p11). What a pity this loco was not preserved instead of having later to restore Barry wrecks of the same class at a much later date. Built at Eastleigh in 1928, 30837 was one of twenty five Maunsell S15s, and was broken up at Cashmores, Newport in September 1966.

The last operational Drummond M7 0-4-4 T No.30053 was used on the LCGB "Surrey Wanderer" rail tour on 5 July 1964. The engine was beautifully turned out for its last outing by Nine Elms Shed, and after its export to the USA has now thankfully returned to active service in the UK on the Swanage Railway. The M7 tanks had soldiered on until May 1964, by which time they were confined to the Lymington and Swanage Branches. The M7 had taken the train up the branch to Purley from Caterham and then visited the Tattenham Corner Branch, having been specially re-instated for one day only to work this special. After arriving at Tattenham Corner terminus the M7 shunts its stock out of the station in order to run round its train, before returning to Victoria with a diversion to Kensington Olympia en route. For engines built between 1887 and 1911 with no significant alterations over the years, the M7s enjoyed a remarkably long career. General withdrawal did not commence until 1957, and the last few engines were not withdrawn until 17 May 1964.